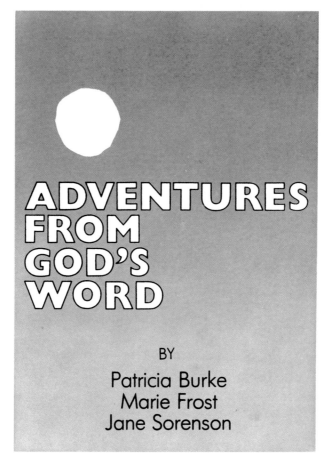

ADVENTURES FROM GOD'S WORD

BY

Patricia Burke
Marie Frost
Jane Sorenson

STANDARD PUBLISHING
Cincinnati, Ohio

2953

Cover Art by Nan Pollard

**Scripture quotations are from the HOLY BIBLE: NEW IN-
TERNATIONAL VERSION, copyright 1978 by the New
York International Bible Society. Used by permission.**

ISBN 0-87239-663-0

The Standard Basic Bible Readers are contemporary editions of the beloved Standard Bible Story Readers, which were written by Lillie A. Faris, and first printed in 1925. More than one and a half million copies of these readers have been used in libraries of homes, schools, and churches.

The favorite Bible stories that forever appeal to children have been rewritten by a team of children's teachers for today's children. All of the illustrations are completely new, drawn by popular Christian artists.

TABLE OF CONTENTS

UNIT THREE:

SEA STORIES

Art by Heidi Petach

UNIT FOUR:

MEETING NEW FRIENDS

Art by Daniel Grossmann

UNIT FIVE:

CHOICES

Art by John Ham

Introduction

Adventures From God's Word is the fourth in a series of Basic Bible Readers especially designed as supplementary reading for third-grade students. Each Bible story has been carefully selected because of its appeal to the middler age. Vocabulary, sentence structure, and sentence length are consistent with public-school guidelines and expectations. The child who is not familiar with Bible words or basic Bible background may enjoy reading the first Standard Basic Bible Readers, Grade One: *I Read About God's Love* and Grade Two: *I Read About God's Care* before reading this book.

Adventures From God's Word is appropriate for reading in the classroom. It may be used for supplementary reading or as a basic text for group reading and understanding.

Adventures From God's Word will be a valuable addition to any library. Certainly it should be included in all church and Christian school libraries as well as in Christian homes.

Adventures From God's Word is divided into units for easy correlation and interest appeal. Grateful acknowledgement is made to the three authors who adapted the stories from the Word of God.

Patricia Anne Burke, who developed the Moving to a New Home unit, has taught English, Bible, and Creative Writing for fourteen years. Her writings have been published in *Decision, Moody Monthly, Vital Christianity, Parents' Magazine, The Upper Room, The English Journal, The Presbyterian Survey,* and *Presbyterian Journal.* A mother and a grandmother, Mrs. Burke has taught Bible stories to children for many years.

Jane Sorenson, who developed the Special Days and Choices units, wrote and bound her first book when she was in the seventh grade. She has taught Creative Writing for Wheaton College and has served as editor for Word, Zondervan, Moody Press, and Christian Advocate. Her articles have appeared in *Christian Life, Eternity,* and *Christian Reader.* Mrs. Sorenson has two children: Sephen, an author-writer-editor, and Linda, who is handicapped and hospitalized.

Marie Frost, who developed the Sea Stories and Making New Friends units, has been writing and editing books and lessons for children for over thirty years. She was the creator of the Peter Panda series, Debbie and Dan, Winky Bear, the Turn-About Twins, Marcy, and many more. Out of her experience as a mother, a grandmother, and a director/teacher of Nursery Schools, Day-care Centers, and Kindergartens, she has also written numerous articles and books such as *Listen to Your Children* for parents and teachers.

—*Marjorie Miller, editor*

Moving

to a New Home

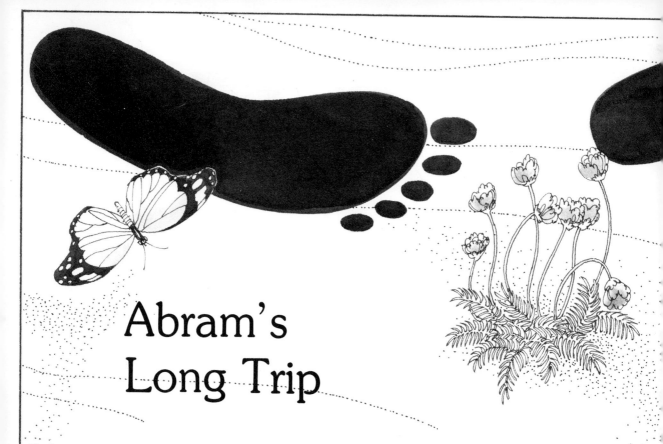

Abram's Long Trip

How would you feel if someone asked you to leave your home and go to a place where you had never been? Suppose you had to leave your family and friends. Would you want to go?

That is what God told Abram to do. "Leave your home and your country," God told Abram, "and go to a land that I will show you. I will make you the father of a great nation. I will bless the whole world through you."

Surely Abram must have been a little afraid, but he did what God told him to do. Of course he took his beautiful wife, Sarai, with him. He also took his nephew, Lot, and his cattle and his helpers. Abram didn't know it, but God was going to do something wonderful for him.

God led Abram to the land of Canaan.

"I'm going to give this land to your children," God told Abram. Now Abram was seventy-five years old, and he didn't even have any children. But he believed God, and he built an altar* at the place where God made this promise to him.

As Abram went on into the land of Canaan, food and water began to get scarce. There was no rain. So Abram had to go down into another land, the land of Egypt. Poor Abram! He still didn't have a home. He must have wondered where God was taking him. But God took care of him and his wife

*Check the glossary on page 126 for the meaning of this word.

and his nephew and his cattle and his helpers. And
when the rain came and there was food again in
Canaan, God led Abram back to the place where he
had built the altar. Abram thanked God for taking
care of him.

Now both Abram and Lot had many servants.
Both had many sheep and cattle. There began to be
trouble. The men who took care of Abram's cattle
and the men who watched over Lot's cattle started
fighting. There just wasn't room for all the animals.

"We can't have this," Abram told Lot. "We're a
family."

"Of course," Lot agreed. "But what can we do?
There is not enough grass to feed all your animals
and mine too."

"Look!" Abram said. "God has said the whole country is ours. Choose any part you want. If you want the left side, I'll take the right. If you want the right, I will be glad to take the land on the left."

Lot looked at the land before him. He studied it very carefully. He saw the rich valley of the Jordan River. There was plenty of water. It looked like a beautiful garden.

"I'll take that," Lot said.

So Lot and his helpers took their cattle down to the beautiful Jordan valley. And Abram and Sarai and their helpers took what was left.

After Lot was gone, God spoke to Abram again. "Take a good look at the land," God told him. "Look in every direction. Look north, south, east, and west. All the land you see will be yours. I am going to give it to you and your children and your children's children and their children.

"You will have many children and grandchildren," God told Abram. "You will have so many that you will not be able to count them. Go now and walk in your new land. Enjoy it. I am giving it all to you."

What wonderful things God had promised to Abram! How excited he must have been! He walked all over his new land. As he walked and looked at the land and thought about God's promises, he was glad he had left his old home. He was happy he had obeyed God.

Abram picked out a place by some oak trees for his tent house. And there he built another altar to God. He wanted to thank God for all He had done for him.

God's promise to Abram was important to him, but it was important to us too. Do you know why? Abram's family grew and grew and grew as God promised it would. And finally, one very special baby was born. That baby was Jesus, the Savior.* Because of Him, the whole world is blessed.*

A Fire
in the Desert

Suppose you were walking along and suddenly a bush caught on fire right before your eyes. But the bush didn't burn up. What would you think? Would you go up for a closer look, or would you run away?

One day Moses was taking care of the sheep for Jethro, his wife's father. He had gone far into the wilderness.* Suddenly Moses saw a strange thing. There was a bush on fire. And in the middle of the bush was an angel.

Moses stared at the bush and the angel. The bush was not burning up, and the angel was not hurt.

"I'll go closer," Moses said. "I want to see why the bush isn't burning up."

As Moses came near the bush, he heard someone calling his name. "Moses, Moses!" the voice said.

"I am here," Moses answered.

"Don't come any closer," the voice said. "Take

your shoes off, Moses. The ground under your feet is holy." The voice was God's. "I am the God of your fathers, Abraham, Isaac, and Jacob," God said.

Moses covered his eyes. He was afraid to look at God.

"Moses," God said, "I have seen the terrible things that are happening to My people in the land of Egypt. I have heard them cry out against their cruel masters.

"I have come to rescue them from the power of the Egyptians. I am going to bring them out of that land and give them a better land, a land flowing with milk and honey.

"Moses," God said, "I'm going to send you to Pharaoh, the king of Egypt. You will bring My

people, the children of Israel, out of the land of Egypt.''

Moses swallowed hard. ''Why me? How can I go to this great Pharaoh and take all those people away from him?''

''I will be with you,'' God answered. ''And I will give you a sign so you will know that I am the one who sent you. After you bring the people out, you will pray and thank God on this very same place where you now stand.''

Moses had another question. ''When the people of Israel ask who You are, what shall I tell them? If I say the God of our fathers sent me, and they ask, 'What is his name?' what do I say?''

''Tell them,'' God said, *''I AM* has sent you. Tell them, 'The God of your fathers, of Abraham,

Isaac, and Jacob, told me to come to you.' This will be my name forever.

"Now go, and tell the wise men of Israel they must meet with you. Say to them, 'The Lord God of your fathers showed himself to me and told me to come to you. He said to tell you He has seen the bad way you are being treated in Egypt.'

"Tell them they have My word that I will rescue them from the cruel men in Egypt and bring them to a land running over with milk and honey.

"The people of Israel will listen to you," God said to Moses. "Take the older men of Israel and go before the king of Egypt. This is what you must say to the king. 'The Lord, the mighty God of Israel has met with us. We need to go into the desert for three days. We want to build an altar there and offer sacrifices* to our God.'

"But the Egyptian king will not let you go," God

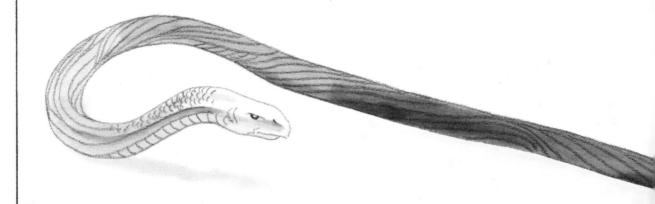

said, "unless a strong hand makes him do it.

"I will stretch out My hand and strike the Egyptians with some wondrous things," God told Moses. "Then the king will let you go."

How happy Moses must have been when he heard these words. His people who had been mistreated by the Egyptians for so long would finally be set free. God would do wonderful things for them.

Moses wanted his people to be free from the cruel Egyptians. But Moses was afraid. How could he, just a man, face the mighty king of Egypt and tell him what God had said? Moses had many things to learn. God, who called himself *I Am*, was more powerful than any king or any army on earth. He would do many wonderful things for Moses and the people of Israel. And He would bring them out of Egypt into the promised land of Canaan.

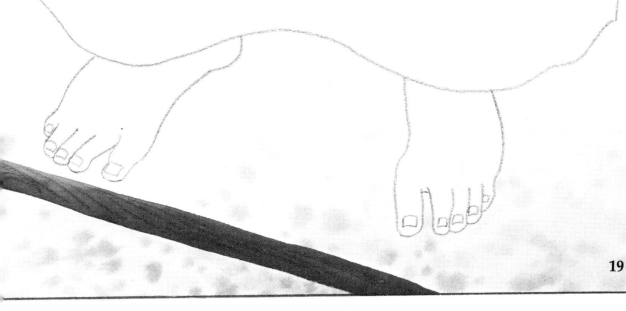

The Spies' Report

The people of Israel were excited. After many long hard years, they had finally come to the edge of Canaan, the land God had promised them. What would their new home be like?

Moses, their leader, went to God at once to find out what to do next. As God spoke to Moses, the people of Israel waited anxiously to hear what He would say.

At last the word came. God told Moses to go to each tribe* of Israel and pick one man to go into Canaan. There were twelve tribes, so twelve men were chosen.

"You are going into the new land to look it over for our people," Moses told the twelve men. "Find out all you can about this new country that God has given us.

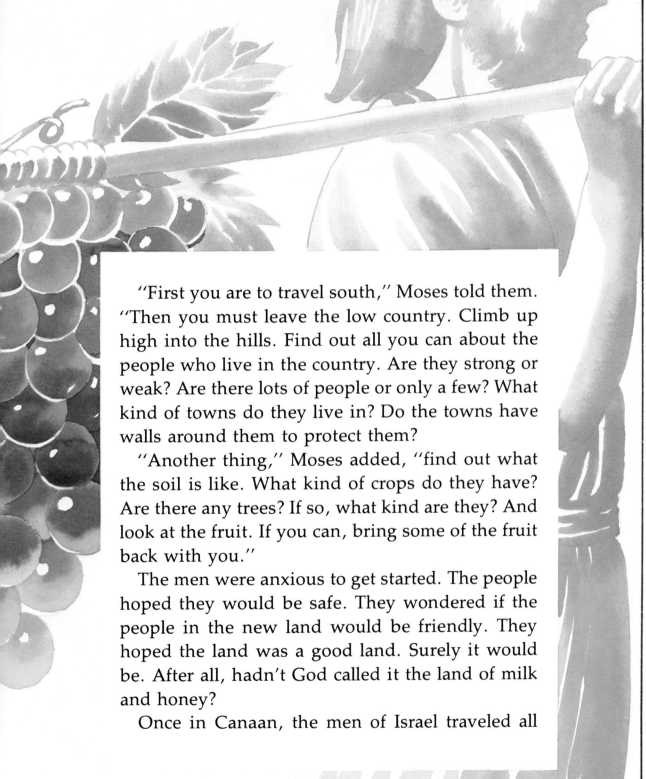

"First you are to travel south," Moses told them. "Then you must leave the low country. Climb up high into the hills. Find out all you can about the people who live in the country. Are they strong or weak? Are there lots of people or only a few? What kind of towns do they live in? Do the towns have walls around them to protect them?

"Another thing," Moses added, "find out what the soil is like. What kind of crops do they have? Are there any trees? If so, what kind are they? And look at the fruit. If you can, bring some of the fruit back with you."

The men were anxious to get started. The people hoped they would be safe. They wondered if the people in the new land would be friendly. They hoped the land was a good land. Surely it would be. After all, hadn't God called it the land of milk and honey?

Once in Canaan, the men of Israel traveled all

21

over the land. They found ripe grapes and pome-granates* and figs in a valley. The grapes were so large that two men carried one bunch, along with some pomegranates and figs, on a pole between them!

The people of Israel waited and waited. Why didn't the men come back? A month went by. The people began to wonder if something had gone wrong.

Finally, after the fortieth day, the men returned.

How glad the people of Israel were! The men looked tired. They showed the people the grapes and other fruit.

"See what we brought back," they said. "The land flows with milk and honey, just as God said it did."

The rest of the men's report was not so good. "Strong people live in the country," they said. "They have large cities. Their cities have high walls. We saw men who were so big they made us look like grasshoppers."

As the men spoke, the people became very frightened. They began to talk among themselves. But Caleb, one of the spies, spoke up. "Quiet!" he said. "God has given us this country. We should go up and take it at once. We are strong enough to do it."

Only one other man, Joshua, agreed with Caleb. The other ten said, "The men in that place are stronger than we are. If we try to fight them, we will all be killed."

The people of Israel believed the ten men who were afraid. They did not believe Caleb and Joshua who said they could take the land. That night, the people cried and said, "Let's choose another leader and go back to Egypt."

The Longest Day

Did you know there was one day that was not like any other in the history of the world? On that day, the sun stood completely still. That was the longest day there has ever been. God made that day long, so the people of Israel could win a great victory over their enemies.

This is how it happened. The people of Israel did not get a new leader and go back to Egypt. But, because they did not trust in God to help them take the land of Canaan, God did not let them go in. Only two people, Joshua and Caleb, were allowed to go. All of the others died in the wilderness.

After Moses died, Joshua was made the new leader. He and Caleb and the children of the people who had not trusted in God went in to make their homes in the land of Canaan.

The news came to the king of Jerusalem that Joshua and the Israelites* had captured the city of Ai, and that the people of another city, Gibeon,

had made friends with the Israelites. This frightened the king. He sent word to five other kings. "Come help me fight and destroy Gibeon," he asked. "Its people are now friends with Joshua and the people of Israel."

The five kings agreed. "Sure. We'll be glad to help you attack Gibeon."

Now it was the people of Gibeon's turn to be afraid. They sent word to Joshua as quickly as they could.

"Help us, Joshua," they begged. "All of the kings in the hill country are joining together to destroy us."

Joshua started right away, with the army of Israel, to help Gibeon. But first, God had a message for Joshua.

"Joshua," God said. "Don't be afraid of all those armies. I will win the battle for you. There will not be one person left to fight you."

Joshua did not waste any time. He traveled all night so he could take the enemy by surprise.

God brought fear to the enemy, so that Joshua's armies killed many of them and chased the others away. God also dropped huge stones of hail upon the enemies' army, so that more died from the hail than from the battle.

But the battle was not over. As Joshua's enemies fled, he prayed to God. Then he said, "Sun, stand still over Gibeon, and moon, you stay in your place as well."

God answered Joshua's prayer. The sun and moon stood still until the army of Israel had time to completely destroy the enemies of God. The people of Israel won a great battle, and not a single one of them died.

Never before or since has there been such a day when the sun and moon stood still. On that long day the people of God won a great victory. And people everywhere knew that there was no God like the God of Israel.

Special Days

Sunday

27

uesday

25

The Passover

The Israelites had been in Egypt for a long time. In the beginning, the kings were nice to them. But as their families grew larger, the Egyptians became afraid. Also, the kings found out they could use God's people to do all the hard work. That is how God's people, the children of Israel, became slaves in Egypt.

God was not happy with this. So He chose Moses to lead His people out of Egypt. Moses wasn't very excited about being picked. He made excuses. But God insisted.

God knew it wouldn't be easy to convince Pharaoh, the king of Egypt, to let His people go. But He promised to do lots of miracles.* Moses' brother Aaron was to go along to do the talking.

"The Lord says you should let His people go.

They want to worship Him in the wilderness," said Moses and Aaron to the Pharaoh.

"Why should I?" Pharaoh asked. "I don't even know who your Lord is. Of course I'm not going to let them go!" And he didn't. In fact, he made the slaves work even harder.

"See, I told you it was useless to talk to Pharaoh," Moses told God. "And now my people are mad at me!"

"You'll see what I can do to a man like Pharaoh," said God. "I am the Lord. I promised to bring My people to a land of their own, and I will. You'll see. Pharaoh will be glad to get rid of you!"

So Moses and his brother went back to Pharaoh. The next time they went, God told them to throw down Aaron's rod in front of Pharaoh. When they did, it became a snake! Pharaoh's magicians turned their rods into snakes too. Their snakes were eaten up by Aaron's. But Pharaoh wouldn't let the people go.

The next miracle God did was even more exciting. Aaron touched the Nile River with his rod. Suddenly all the water in the country turned bright red. It was blood! No one could drink it. Even the fish died. Pharaoh's magicians did the same thing. So the king said, "Big deal! The people can't go!"

A week later, Moses told Pharaoh that unless he let the people go, the land would be filled with frogs. The magicians produced frogs too.

By now, Pharaoh was getting tired of having frogs all over the place. He promised he'd let God's people go the next day. But once the frogs were dead, he changed his mind.

Next, God had Aaron hit the ground with his rod to make lice* fill the country. When the magicians tried to do this, they couldn't do it.

"You'd better listen," they told Pharaoh. "God made this happen."

But Pharaoh wouldn't change his mind. God sent swarms of flies and disease* to all the Egyptian cows and horses and sheep. He made terrible sores come on the skin of all the Egyptians and their animals. He sent hail, and fire, and locusts* so that all the Egyptians' crops were destroyed. Still, Pharaoh wouldn't let God's people go. Sometimes he said he would, but as soon as the problems were over, he changed his mind.

At last God told Moses of His final plan. The people listened carefully as Moses explained what would happen.

"In the middle of the night, the angel of death will visit all of Egypt. The oldest child and the oldest animal in every family will die.

"Listen carefully to what God wants you to do. On the tenth day of this month, each family must set aside a perfect lamb. Keep it until the fourteenth day. That evening all the men will kill the lambs.

"Then each family must take some of the lamb's blood and put it on the sides and top of the doorframe of their house. Roast the lamb and eat it, along with bitter herbs* and bread made without yeast.

"When you eat your meal, be fully dressed and ready to go."

Moses continued to speak. "This is going to be called the Feast of the Passover. When the angel of death sees the blood on your doors, he will skip your house, and your children and animals won't die. The angel will *pass over* your houses."

God's people did what God told them to do. None of them died. But all over Egypt people were crying. The death angel had stopped at every house that did not have blood on the door!

Pharaoh called Moses and Aaron while it was still dark. "Get going!" he said. "Take your cattle and sheep and go!"

The Israelites left in a hurry, taking with them silver and gold given to them by the Egyptians. The Lord went in front of them to show them the way. In the daytime, He was in a cloud. At night, He was in a flame of fire.

One night the Israelites were camping by the Red Sea when they heard the sound of chariots.* Pharaoh had changed his mind again and was coming after them.

The people had never been so scared! The Egyptians were coming after them, and the Red Sea was in front of them.

"Hold up your rod over the water," God told Moses. Moses held up his rod. The water formed two walls with dry land between. All the Israelites walked right through to the other side.

When the Egyptians tried to follow, God told Moses to stretch his hand out again. The sea returned to its bed, and the Egyptians were drowned.

God wanted His people never to forget how He led them out of Egypt. He told them to celebrate the Passover every year and remember how He had saved them.

God Gives the Ten Commandments

The Johnson family lived in a house on the corner. When they first moved in, not many cars passed by their house. But, as the town grew, traffic increased. Soon cars meeting at the corner began to have accidents. A traffic signal was put up. Drivers who obeyed the signal were safe.

People need rules to help them live safe and

happy lives. Families have rules to teach children the difference between right and wrong.

God knew that His people needed rules in order to get along with each other. His rules would help the people know how they could please Him too.

Three months after their escape from Egypt, the Israelites were camping at the foot of Mt. Sinai. Moses went up to talk with God. God called to him saying, "I want you to remind the people that I was the one who brought them out of Egypt. They are My special people. They will always be My special

people. But they must obey Me and follow My rules."

When Moses told the people what God said, they were happy. "We will do everything God says we should do," they said.

But the people didn't know what God's rules were yet. They had three days to pray and get ready. They wondered what would happen.

On the morning of the third day, the people watched. There was thunder and lightning. A thick cloud covered the top of the mountain. Suddenly the air was filled with a loud trumpet blast. The people were so scared they shook.

God called to Moses from the top of the mountain. "Come on up, and bring your brother. Tell the people to wait down there."

On the mountain, God told Moses many rules for living a life that would please Him. Ten rules were so important they were called the Ten Commandments. Sometimes they are called God's Law.

The Ten Commandments showed the people that God expected to have first place in their lives. He alone was to be worshiped and obeyed. The Commandments told the people they were to treat other people with love and respect.

When the people heard God's Law, they said, "We will do everything He said. We will trust Him. We want the blessing He has promised."

Moses wrote down all the words of God. He built an altar at the foot of the mountain. The people sacrificed oxen as peace offerings to God. Half of the blood from the animals was put in big bowls. The rest was sprinkled on the altar.

Once again Moses read God's Law to the people. And once again they said, "All that God has said, we will do."

Then Moses took the bowls and sprinkled the rest of the blood on the people. This was to remind them that their agreement with God was sealed in blood.

The people remembered that God told them to put blood on their doors the night they got out of Egypt. Because of the blood, the death angel had passed over their houses, and they were safe.

God called Moses to come up on the mountain again. While he was there, God gave him the Commandments which He had written on tablets of stone.

Jesus and the Commandments

When Jesus came to earth, He often looked back at Mt. Sinai and the laws received there. He talked about these laws and included most of them in His own teaching.

One day a rich young ruler came to see Jesus. The Bible does not tell us his name, or why he was called a ruler. But he must have been important, and he was rich.

This young man asked a very important question: "What must I do to have eternal life?" He wanted to have the hope of living in Heaven some day, and he thought Jesus would have the answer.

Jesus quoted some of the Old Testament Commandments given at Mt. Sinai. "Do not commit adultery. Do not kill. Do not steal. Do not bear false witness. Honor thy father and thy mother."

The rich young ruler said, "I have obeyed these laws since I was a child."

Wouldn't it be wonderful to be able to truthfully say, "I obey all the laws of God"?

Then Jesus said, "You will need to do one thing. You must give away your money, so you can have riches in Heaven. Come, follow Me."

Jesus did not ask all followers to give up their wealth, only those who would let it have first place in their lives. God must have first place in every life.

The Ten Commandments

And God spoke all these words:

"I am the Lord your God, who brought you out of Egypt, out of the land of slavery.

You shall have no other gods before me.

You shall not make for yourself an idol in the form of anything in heaven above or on the earth beneath or in the waters below. You shall not bow down to them or worship them; for I, the Lord your God, am a jealous God, punishing the children for the sin of the fathers to the third and fourth generation of those who hate me, but showing love to thousands who love me and keep my commandments.

You shall not misuse the name of the Lord your God, for the Lord will not hold anyone guiltless who misuses his name.

Remember the Sabbath day by keeping it holy. Six days you shall labor and do all your work, but the seventh day is a Sabbath to the Lord your God. On it you shall not do any work, neither you, nor your son or daughter, nor your manservant or maidservant, nor your animals, nor the alien within your gates. For in six days the Lord made the heavens and the earth, the sea, and all that is in them, but he rested on the seventh day. Therefore the Lord blessed the Sabbath day and made it holy.

Honor your father and your mother, so that you may live long in the land the Lord your God is giving you.

You shall not murder.

You shall not commit adultery.

You shall not steal.

You shall not give false testimony against your neighbor.

You shall not covet your neighbor's house. You shall not covet your neighbor's wife, or his manservant or maidservant, his ox or donkey, or anything that belongs to your neighbor."

Exodus 20:1-17.

The Feast of Tabernacles

Sometimes, as time goes by, the reason for having a holiday is forgotten. When the Pilgrims celebrated the first Thanksgiving, it was a time to thank God for safety and harvest. Now some people think of Thanksgiving as a day off from school, or a big dinner with stuffed turkey, cranberries, and pie.

The Israelites had a special day very much like our Thanksgiving. It was called the Feast of Tabernacles.*

Rules for the Feast of Tabernacles were given to Moses at the time God gave him the Commandments. At the end of the year, when God's people harvested their crops, they were commanded to have a special celebration.

But as the years went by, the people forgot about the celebration. By the time Nehemiah was governor, the people hadn't heard the Law for a long time. They didn't remember what God had told them. As God's Commandments were read, they felt very sad.

"This is a day of celebration," Nehemiah told them. "Be happy. The joy of the Lord will make you strong."

As the people listened to God's Word, they realized they had forgotten how to celebrate the Feast of Tabernacles.

God had told them to make little booths* out of leafy branches. They were to stay in the booths and listen to their leader read God's Law. They hadn't done this in years! But now they went to gather the branches and make their little booths.

Just as God commanded, they stayed inside their booths for seven days. And every day they listened to the reading of the Law.

Now the people really were happy. They understood God's Word. They thanked Him for caring for them.

Jesus' Birthday

"What do you want for Christmas?" "Who will help decorate the tree?" "Where is the wrapping paper?" "I haven't finished my shopping." "Did we send them a card?"

Sometimes we get so busy at Christmastime that we almost forget why we celebrate Christmas. It is Jesus' birthday!

The Roman king had made a rule that everyone had to sign up in the city where his family had lived. That's why Mary and Joseph went to Bethlehem. It was time for Mary's baby to be born. An angel had told her that she would be the mother of God's Son.

When Mary and Joseph got to Bethlehem, the town was full of people. Joseph tried to find a room for them, but everybody said, "Sorry. All our rooms are taken." The only place they could find to sleep was a barn.

That night Mary's baby was born. There was no hospital, no doctor, no nurse. But Jesus was born anyway—right in that barn. Mary wrapped the baby in soft cloths and laid Him in a manger.

In a field not far away, some shepherds were taking care of their sheep. Suddenly an angel stood in front of them. The angel was shining like a great light. The shepherds were scared stiff!

"Don't be afraid," said the angel. "I won't hurt you. I have good news for you and for all people everywhere. Just now, in Bethlehem over there, a baby was born. This baby is the Savior you've been waiting for."

The shepherds listened carefully.

"This is how you will know Him," the angel said. "He's wrapped in cloths and lying in a manger in a barn!"

All of a sudden the sky seemed to be filled with angels. They were praising God and saying, "Glory to God in the highest, and on earth peace among people who love God."

The angels were gone as suddenly as they had come.

"Well," said the shepherds, "let's go see Him!"

They hurried to Bethlehem and found Him just as the angel had said they would. There were Mary and Joseph. And there was the baby. How happy the shepherds were! They returned to their fields praising God. And they told everybody they saw what the angels had said. Mary remembered every word and thought about that night over and over again.

The shepherds weren't the only strangers who saw the baby Jesus. He was also visited by some Wise-men.

These Wise-men had read many books. They had studied the stars. And they were watching for a sign of the Savior's birth. Suddenly they saw a very special star in the east. They knew this was the sign they had been looking for.

The Wise-men followed the star to Jerusalem. Surely a king would be born in the city of Jerusalem, they thought. And surely everybody in Jerusalem would know about the baby. So they stopped to ask where they would find Him. "Can you tell us where we can find the King of the Jews?" they asked.

King Herod heard about it. He asked around to see if anyone knew what was going on.

"The Scriptures say the Savior will be born in Bethlehem," the king was told.

"Tell me," King Herod asked the Wise-men, "when did you first see the star? I'd like to go and worship the baby king too. Go to Bethlehem and find Him. When you do, come back and tell me where He is. I want to go and worship Him, too."

The Wise-men went on toward Bethlehem. The star which they had seen in the east went ahead of them to show the way. At last it stopped over the spot where Jesus lay.

By this time, most of the people who had come to Bethlehem to sign up had gone back home. And Jesus and Mary and Joseph were living in a house. The Wise-men were thrilled* to find them! They knelt down and worshiped the baby. They gave Mary expensive gifts for Jesus—gold and valuable spices.

Now God knew that King Herod did not really want to worship Jesus. He wanted to kill Him. So God told the Wise-men in a dream not to go back through Jerusalem, but to go home another way.

Mary named her baby Jesus. God had told her to name Him Jesus. He would save people from their sins. Sometimes He is called Emanuel, which means "God with us." This little baby was the Son of God.

Mary and Joseph looked at the gifts the Wise-men had brought to Jesus. They were very expensive, worth lots of money! What should they do with them? Should they sell the gold, frankincense, and myrrh and use the money for things Jesus needed? Or should they put them away and save

them for later use? What would you have done with the gifts?

That night in a dream, an angel of God talked to Joseph and said, "Joseph, get up right now and leave Bethlehem. Take Mary and Jesus and hurry as fast as you can to the country of Egypt. King Herod will try to find Jesus and kill Him, but you will be safe in Egypt. Stay and live there until I tell you to leave."

Just as quietly as they could, Joseph, Mary, and young Jesus left their home.

"We will be safe in Egypt," said Joseph. "Herod won't be able to find us. We will be too far away."

"How long will we be in Egypt?" asked Mary.

"Until God tells us it is safe to leave," answered Joseph. "I don't know how long, Mary. But God will take care of us."

Mary and Joseph and Jesus lived in Egypt until King Herod died. Then when Herod could no longer harm Jesus, an angel of God appeared in a dream and told Joseph, "It is time for you to return home from Egypt. Herod is dead."

King for a Day

Jennifer was thrilled* to be chosen for the queen's court for the Fourth of July parade. When they put the golden crown on her head which showed she was queen, she was so happy she almost cried. Of course, she got to ride in a convertible* down Main Street. She smiled and waved. Everybody along the street cheered.

But popularity* doesn't always last. The next day, without her crown, Jennifer looked just like the other girls. Nobody cheered when she went by. Even stars in sports and entertainment often find that other people have taken their places.

Near the end of His life, Jesus was "King for a Day." We celebrate that day the Sunday before Resurrection* Day. Some people call this day Palm Sunday.

Jesus and His disciples* were near Jerusalem just before the time of the Passover Feast. (Do you remember what that celebrated?)

"You two," Jesus said, motioning, "go over to that village* across the way. As you enter town, you'll see a colt tied. No one has ever ridden the colt. Untie it and bring it to me."

"What if the owners try to stop us?" one disciple asked.

"Just say the Lord needs it, and He will send it right back."

The two men entered the village. Just as Jesus had said, there was the colt. They untied it.

"Hey, what do you think you're doing?" asked the people standing by.

The disciples just looked at the people and said what Jesus had told them to say. "The Lord needs it, and He will bring it right back," they said.

"Okay," said the people, "good enough."

So the disciples took the colt to Jesus. They didn't have a saddle, so they threw their coats over the colt's back for Jesus to sit on.

Jesus and His disciples traveled into Jerusalem. People were standing and waiting for them. Some of the people threw down their coats along the road. Some spread palm branches or waved them like flags.

"Hurrah for the King!" people shouted.

It was like a little parade.

But some people didn't like it.

"What kind of king is that?" they whispered. "We expected a king on a big horse. A real king would wear a gold crown. This man doesn't look like a king to us!"

Jesus knew that His kingdom would be different. He came to be a servant, not an earthly ruler.

The crowds kept shouting, "Hosanna!* Blessed is He who comes in the name of the Lord! Here comes the king!"

As Jesus rode along on the colt's back, He knew His popularity wouldn't last. He knew that before the week was over, the people would be shouting for His death.

Jesus Goes Back to Heaven

Saying good-bye is sometimes hard to do. Jesus had told His friends that He would be going away. But they had a hard time understanding.

Jesus said He had come to do His Father's work. He taught and healed people. He also came to be the Lamb of God—to take away the sins of the world. He came to earth to die.

Jesus was not surprised when evil men decided to kill Him. The perfect lamb in Egypt was killed. And its blood saved those who believed.

But Jesus was not like any other lamb—or any other person. After He was crucified,* dead, and buried, He became alive again on the third day! That is the holiday we celebrate as Resurrection Day. Some people call it Easter.

After Jesus became alive again, for forty days He met with His friends. He ate with them. He talked with them. He taught them. Thousands of people saw Him alive.

"I'm going to get a place ready for you," Jesus had told His friends. "I want you to be with Me forever. You can't come now, but I'll be back."

Now the time had come for them to say good-bye. They stood together on a small mountain.

"I want you to do something for Me," Jesus told His friends. "Go everywhere and tell others about Me. Teach them the lessons I have taught you. And don't forget that My Spirit* will always be with you!''

As the disciples watched, Jesus rose up and disappeared into a cloud.

Suddenly two men in white robes appeared. ''Why are you standing here looking up?'' they asked. ''Jesus, who just went up to Heaven, will come back the same way He left.''

Jesus' friends remembered that He had told them He would come again. So it wasn't good-bye forever. Now they must tell other people about Him.

Sea Stories

Jonah and
the Big Fish

"Jonah," God said, "go to the city of Nineveh. Tell the people to stop disobeying Me and doing bad things."

Jonah did not want to obey God. "I will run away on a big ship," Jonah said to himself. "Then I won't have to go to Nineveh."

But God knew where Jonah was. God knows everything.

As the ship sailed out to sea, God sent a big storm. The wind was so strong and the waves were so high, the ship was ready to crash.

The sailors were afraid. "The ship will sink!" they said. "We must throw everything we can into the sea. Maybe then we can row the ship."

They threw everything they could spare into the sea. But the storm got even worse. God was going to show Jonah that he must obey.

Now Jonah was sleeping in the bottom of the ship.

"Why are you sleeping?" asked the captain. "Get up and pray to your God."

"I am running away from God," said Jonah. "He sent this big storm because of me."

"So this is *your* fault," said the sailors. "What should we do to you so your God will stop the storm?"

"Throw me into the sea, and the storm will stop," said Jonah.

"Oh, we don't want to do that," said the sailors. And they rowed even harder. But the storm got worse and worse.

The sailors prayed to God to forgive them. Then they picked Jonah up and threw him into the sea.

The storm stopped.

As Jonah fell toward the sea, a big fish jumped up and swallowed him.

"I'm going to die," Jonah thought.

But he didn't. God took care of him. God had

made a special fish. Jonah stayed alive inside the fish for three days.

Jonah did not like being inside the fish. He prayed, "Dear God, please help me. I am sorry I did not obey. I promise to do what You want me to do."

God heard Jonah. He made the fish spit Jonah out onto the shore.

"Thank You, God," said Jonah. "I will go to the city and tell the people what You want me to tell them."

The people listened to Jonah. "We are sorry we did wrong," they said. "We will be good now. Maybe God will not be angry with us anymore."

God was glad the people were going to be good. "I will not destroy their city," He said.

This made Jonah angry. He went out of the city and sat under a shade tree. God made the tree die. Now Jonah was even more angry.

"Why are you angry?" God asked. "These people are sorry they did wrong. Shouldn't I forgive them?"

Can you think of somebody else God forgave?

A Chariot of Fire

Elijah was a prophet. He had spent his life telling people what God wanted them to know, and God had taken care of him. One time when Elijah had to hide from King Ahab, God sent birds to bring him bread and meat to eat.

Another time, God sent fire from Heaven to burn up Elijah's sacrifice and prove that He was God. Now Elijah was getting old. His work for God was almost done.

Elijah had a young helper named Elisha. Elijah told Elisha, "When I am no longer here, you will do my work." So Elisha went with Elijah and helped him wherever he went.

One day Elijah said to Elisha, "Stay here while I go down to the town of Bethel."

"I won't leave you ever!" said Elisha. So Elijah and Elisha walked together to Bethel.

When they got to Bethel, Elijah said to Elisha, "Please stay here. God has told me to go to Jericho."

"I will not leave you," said Elisha. So Elijah and Elisha walked together to Jericho.

When they got to Jericho, Elijah said to Elisha, "Please stay here. God is sending me to the Jordan River."

And once again, Elisha said, "I will not leave you."

When they got to the Jordan River, Elijah took off his coat and hit the water with it. God made a path right through the water! Elijah and Elisha walked across on dry land.

When Elijah and Elisha got to the other side, Elijah said, "I'm going to leave you very soon, and you cannot go with me. But before I go, I want to do something for you. What should it be?"

Elisha thought of all the wonderful things God had helped Elijah do. Finally he answered, "I would like to have twice as much of God's power as you have."

"You have asked a hard thing," said Elijah, "but if you see me when I leave, you will have what you ask. If not, your wish will not be granted."

Elijah and Elisha kept walking and talking. Then suddenly a great wind started to blow. Horses pulling a chariot of fire came down from Heaven! The chariot came right between Elijah and Elisha. Then it went up into Heaven carrying Elijah.

Elisha watched the chariot disappear. Then he reached down and picked something up. It was Elijah's coat. It had fallen to the ground as Elijah went up in the chariot. Elisha went back to the Jordan River. He hit the water with Elijah's coat. "Where are You, God?" said Elisha.

God heard Elisha. He made a dry path through the water for Elisha to walk on. Elisha knew that God had granted his wish. He was ready to take Elijah's place and tell people what God wanted them to know.

Shipwreck!

Paul was on a prison ship headed for Rome. He had been in prison many times before. And he had been on ships before. But he had never been to Rome.

Paul had not done anything wrong. He had been put in prison because he preached about Jesus. Now he was going to Rome to be judged by Caesar, the greatest ruler in all the land.

Paul was not afraid. He knew God would take care of him. And he was looking forward to talking with Caesar and telling him about Jesus.

The guard who was in charge of Paul was good to him. When the ship stopped at towns along the way, he let Paul get off the ship to visit with his Christian friends.

The ship traveled very slowly. The weather was not good for sailing, and winter would be coming soon. One day the waves were so high and the winds blew so hard that the captain brought the ship into a port. "This place is not a good place to spend the winter," the captain said. "We'll stay here a few days. Then we will set out to sea again."

Paul disagreed with the captain. "We should not go on," Paul said. "If we do, our ship will surely get wrecked. You will lose the things you are taking to Rome. We may lose our lives too."

The pilot, the captain, and the other people who

were in charge of the ship listened to Paul. They talked it over. Then they took a vote. Most of them wanted to go on to a larger place before stopping for the winter.

"I think we can make it to Phoenix," the captain said. "That would be a better place. As soon as a good south wind comes along, we'll get going."

It wasn't long before the right kind of wind came. "Hurrah!" shouted the people as they started sailing along close to the shore.

But the nice south wind didn't last long! Instead, a northeastern wind began to blow. It caught the ship up and took it out to sea. The pilot tried to keep the ship on its course. But he couldn't, so he gave up and let it drift with the wind.

The next day the winds were even stronger and the waves were even higher.

"Throw whatever you can overboard. Maybe that will help," said the captain. So they threw everything they could into the sea.

Still the storm didn't stop. The next day they threw the ropes and chains they used on the ship into the sea. Day after day the terrible storm went on. It was so bad they couldn't even see the sun in the daytime or the stars at night. They were so worried they couldn't eat or sleep. "We're all going to die in the storm," they said.

Finally Paul spoke up. "If you had listened to me," he said, "we wouldn't be in this mess. But it could be worse. The ship will be wrecked, but none of us will die. Last night an angel of God spoke to me and told me not to be afraid. God wants me to stand before Caesar in Rome. He has promised that no one in this ship will die."

As the days and nights went on, the sailors could tell they were getting closer to shore. They were afraid the ship would crash on the rocks. So one night, they let the lifeboat into the sea, and were starting to climb down into it.

Paul saw them.

"If they leave," he told the guards, "you will die." So the sailors cut the ropes to the lifeboat and it fell into the sea.

The next morning Paul told the people to eat.

"You haven't eaten for two weeks. You need food. Remember, you are not going to die." Paul gave thanks for the food and began to eat. The people felt better. All of them had something to eat.

That afternoon the ship hit some rocks and began to break into pieces. The soldiers wanted to kill the prisoners so they would not swim away and escape. But Paul's guard stopped them saying, "Those of you who can swim, jump overboard and swim to shore. The rest of you can grab a board or something and float to shore."

Just as God had promised, everyone came safely to shore. How glad they were to be on land once again! Kind people were waiting for them as they came out of the sea. They built a fire for them so they could get warm and dry.

Paul picked up some sticks and laid them on the fire. Everyone watched as a very poisonous snake came out of the fire and crawled up on Paul's hand. Would the snake bite Paul? Would Paul die?

Paul shook the snake off into the fire. The people were surprised that Paul was not hurt.

Paul and the others stayed on the island the rest of the winter. The people on the island were good to them. When they found a ship that was leaving for Rome, the people gave them food and other things they would need for the trip.

As Paul sailed on to Rome, he thanked God for taking care of him.

Jesus Walks on the Water

It had been a long day. Jesus had taught the people how to please God and be happy. He had healed sick people. He had fed the people. Now it was time to go home.

"I will stay here and say good-bye to the people," Jesus told His disciples. "You get in the boat and row back home."

After all the people left, Jesus went up to the mountain to pray. But the disciples were having a hard time. They were in the middle of the sea in the middle of the night when a big storm came up. A strong wind began to blow. Angry waves hit against the boat. One of Jesus' disciples tried to steer the boat, but he couldn't.

Jesus knows everything. He knew the disciples were in trouble.

Because Jesus is the Son of God, He can do wonderful things. He started toward the boat walking right on top of the water.

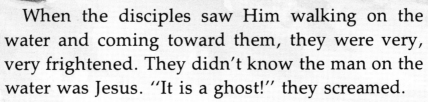

When the disciples saw Him walking on the water and coming toward them, they were very, very frightened. They didn't know the man on the water was Jesus. "It is a ghost!" they screamed.

"Don't be afraid," Jesus said. "It is I."

"If it's really You," Peter said, "tell me to come to You on the water."

"Come," Jesus said.

Peter got out of the boat and began to walk on the water toward Jesus. Suddenly Peter began to be afraid. And he began to sink. But Jesus reached out His hand and lifted Peter up. Together they walked toward the boat. When they climbed into the boat, the wind stopped blowing and the waves stopped splashing.

The disciples didn't know what to think. But they knew one thing.

"You are God's Son!" they said to Jesus.

The disciples should not have been so surprised. They had seen Jesus do many miracles. They had just seen Him change five little loaves of bread and two fishes into lots and lots of food to feed thousands of people. But they still could not understand. They rowed to the other side of the lake still wondering about Jesus and His power.

Meeting New Friends

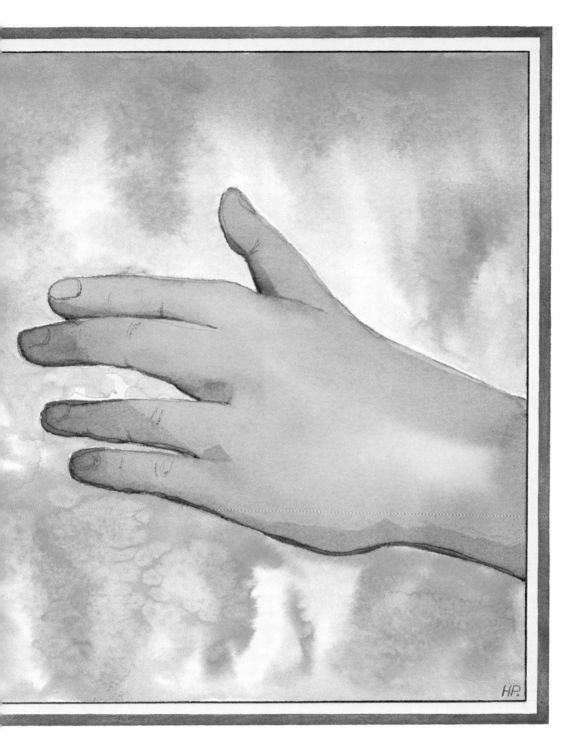

Philip and the Ethiopian

The church in Jerusalem was growing. The enemies of the church were growing too. They were going into the houses of the Christians and dragging them off to prison.

Some of the Christians were killed. Others left the city and went to different places. One of the Christians who left Jerusalem was a man named Philip.

Philip went down to Samaria and began to tell the people there about Jesus. The people listened to what Philip said. They saw him heal the sick. Many of them believed in Jesus and were baptized.

There was great happiness in the city because Philip had shared the good news of Jesus with them.

But God had other plans for Philip. He sent an angel to tell Philip what to do. "I want you to take the desert* road that leads to Gaza," the angel told him.

Philip must have wondered why he should go to a lonely road where there were hardly any people. But he obeyed God and started.

While he was walking down the road, Philip heard a chariot coming. An important man was riding in the chariot. The man was in charge of all the money belonging to the queen of Ethiopia.

God told Philip to go and talk to the Ethiopian. So Philip ran along the side of the chariot. Philip saw that the man was reading the Bible.

"Do you understand what you are reading?"
Philip asked.

"How can I understand when there is no one to
explain the words to me?" the man said. "Get in
the chariot with me. Maybe you can help me understand the words."

The words that the man was reading were about
Jesus.

"Who is this about?" the man asked.

"This is about Jesus," Philip said. Then Philip
told the man all about Jesus. He told him how Jesus
loves everyone. He told him that Jesus died on the
cross to save people from their sins. He told him
that Jesus rose from the dead. He told him that
Jesus is in Heaven with God.

As Philip talked to the man, the man began to

understand. He believed in Jesus. He wanted to do
what Jesus wanted him to do.

"Look!" the Ethiopian said, as they came to a
lake. "Here is some water. I want to be baptized.*"

They stopped the chariot. Philip and the Ethiopian went down into the water, and Philip baptized him.

When Philip and the Ethiopian came up out of
the water, the Ethiopian got back in the chariot. He
had never been so happy in his life. Now he understood what he had read. Now he knew about
Jesus. He knew Jesus loved him.

Philip was happy too. He was glad God had sent
him to tell the Ethiopian about Jesus. He hoped the
man would tell the queen and all his friends about
Jesus.

The Christians Help Saul

Saul was an angry young man. He believed in God. He prayed to God. He obeyed God's laws. But he did not believe Jesus was God's Son. Saul thought that the followers of Jesus, the Christians,* were wrong. He wanted to kill all the Christians in the world. Then there would be no one left who believed Jesus was the Son of God. He believed that this was what God wanted him to do.

One day Saul was walking along the road to Damascus. He was going there to look for Christians. He would put the Christians in prison. As Saul walked along, he was making threats. "Those Christians will wish they had never heard of

Jesus," he said. "Just wait till I get my hands on them!"

Just then a bright light from Heaven flashed around him. The light was so bright that he covered his eyes and fell to the ground. Then he heard a voice say, "Saul, Saul, why are you fighting Me?"

"Who are you, Lord?" Saul asked.

The voice said, "I am Jesus, the one you are fighting against. Get up off the ground and go on into the city of Damascus. Wait there until you are told what you must do."

The men who were with Saul didn't know what to think. "We heard a voice speak, but we didn't see anyone," they said.

Saul got up from the ground. He opened his eyes, but he couldn't see. His friends had to lead him into the city.

When they got to Damascus, Saul was still blind. For three days he didn't eat or drink anything. He needed to think about what had happened. He couldn't understand it. He prayed to God to help him know and do what was right.

Now there was a Christian man named Ananias who lived in Damascus. God came to Ananias and told him to go to Saul. "Go to the home of Judas on Straight Street and ask for Saul," God said. "He is praying. I have told him you are coming. You will lay your hands on him and make him see again."

Ananias wasn't sure he wanted to help Saul. "I

have heard about the terrible things this man has done to Christians," Ananias said. "He has come here to find Christians and put them in prison."

"Go," God told Ananias. "I have chosen this man for a special work. He will tell many people in many countries about Me. He will even get to tell kings about Me. And he will be hated and hunted and hurt because of Me."

So Ananias went to Saul. "Brother Saul," he said, "Jesus has sent me to you. He wants you to see again. And He wants you to have the Holy Spirit in your life."

Suddenly Saul could see again. He was baptized. Now Saul was a Christian too!

Saul was happy. Instead of killing the Christians, he began to tell people about Jesus. Everywhere he went he told people, "Jesus is the Son of God."

When the people heard Saul, they couldn't believe their ears. "Isn't this the same man who used to hunt for Christians so he could put them in jail? Isn't that why he came to Damascus? What has happened to him?"

Saul's old friends were surprised too. And they were very angry. Now that Saul believed that Jesus was God's Son, he worked as hard for Him as he had worked against Him. Many people became Christians because of Saul's preaching and his changed life.

"We have to get rid of this man," the Jews said. "Too many people believe what he says. If we don't stop him, all the people in the city are going to become Christians." Then they thought of a plan. They put spies at every gate of the city. "When he leaves the city," they said, "we will catch him and kill him."

Saul's friends heard about the plan. They knew the Jews would kill Saul. They must think of something. How could they get Saul out of the city without his enemies knowing it?

All of Saul's friends were trying to think of some way to get him out of the city without going through one of the gates. They prayed about it. Then someone had an idea.

One night, they put Saul in a big basket. They tied a strong rope to the basket. Then they carefully pushed the basket through a window in the wall, and let it slowly down to the ground.

Saul's enemies never saw him at all. How surprised they were when they heard he was in Jerusalem!

But everything was not well in Jerusalem either. The Christians there were afraid of Saul. They thought he was just pretending to believe in Jesus. They remembered how mean he had been before. They were afraid he was trying to trick them so he could catch them and put them in prison. Barnabas was one of the Christians in Jerusalem. He heard about how Saul saw Jesus on the road to Damascus. He heard how Saul preached about Jesus in Damascus. He wanted to be Saul's friend.

"This man has really changed," Barnabas told the Christians. "He is one of us now."

The Christians listened to Barnabas. What he said was true. Saul talked like a Christian. He acted like a Christian too. He was kind and good, not mean and angry the way he had been before.

"We believe you," they told Saul. "We want to be your friends too. Let's all work together for Jesus."

Two Prisoners
and a Jailer

Sometime after Saul became a Christian, his name was changed to Paul. Paul and his friend Silas went to Macedonia to tell the people there about Jesus. One day as Paul and Silas were going to a place to pray, a slave girl started following them and shouting, "These men are servants of God. They will tell you how to be saved." Day after day she did this.

Paul knew the girl had an evil spirit. The spirit told her things that were going to happen. Some greedy men knew this too. They were making money by having people pay to hear what the girl would tell them.

One day Paul turned to the girl and said to the evil spirit, "In the name of Jesus, come out of her." That very minute, the spirit left.

The girl was happy. But the greedy men were angry. They grabbed Paul and Silas and dragged them before the judges. "These men are not obeying your law," the bad men said.

So Paul and Silas were whipped and thrown into jail. And their feet were fastened with chains so they could not walk.

Paul and Silas could have cried and felt sorry for themselves. But they didn't. They prayed and sang songs to God.

That night while they were singing and praying, God sent a big earthquake.*

Bang went the prison doors. *Crash* went the chains as they fell off the prisoners' feet. Every door was open. Paul and Silas and all the other prisoners were free to escape.

The noise woke the jailer in charge of the prisoners. He saw the open doors. He was sure everyone had run away.

"I will be killed if the prisoners are gone," he cried. "I will kill myself."

"No! Don't hurt yourself. We are all here!" Paul shouted.

The jailer lit a lamp and looked. Paul was telling the truth. All of the prisoners were there. He knew Paul and Silas were Christians. He knew God had sent the earthquake.

Shaking with fear, the jailer fell on his knees before Paul and Silas. "Sirs, what must I do to be saved?" he asked.

"Believe that Jesus is the Son of God," Paul and Silas answered. "You and your whole family can be saved."

Paul and Silas went to the jailer's house. The jailer washed and doctored their hurt backs. Paul and Silas told all the jailer's family about Jesus. They believed Jesus was God's Son. They were sorry for their sins. Paul and Silas baptized everybody in the jailer's family. How happy they were! They brought food for Paul and Silas, and listened

as they talked and sang songs about Jesus.

The next morning the judges sent some policemen to get Paul and Silas out of jail.

"No way!" said Paul. "They whipped us in public. They threw us in jail when we had done nothing wrong. Now they send policemen to let us out in secret. We won't go until they come."

When the judges heard that, they were afraid. They came to the jail. "Please leave," they begged. "Please leave our city. We don't want you here."

So Paul and Silas said good-bye to their friends. Then they went on to another city and told more people about Jesus.

A Queen Visits a Wise King

King Solomon was a young man. He loved God very much. He wanted to be a good king. But he knew it was very hard to be a good king. There were many things a king needed to know.

One night Solomon had a dream. God said, "Solomon, if you could have one thing, what would you want Me to give you?"

"You were kind to my father, David, because he was a good king, and he obeyed You," Solomon answered. "Now I am king in his place. I don't always know the right thing to do. Help me to be understanding and to know right from wrong."

God was pleased with what Solomon asked for. "I will give you an understanding heart," He promised. "I will also make you rich and powerful."

God kept His promise. King Solomon became the richest and wisest man in the world.

At the same time, there was a queen who lived in the country of Sheba. She was also wise and rich.

"I don't believe anybody is as wise and rich as people say King Solomon is," said the queen. "I will go and see for myself. I will ask him hard questions and see if he knows the answers."

So the queen went to see King Solomon. She took with her many camels, spices, gold, and jewels to give as presents to the king. And she asked King Solomon the hardest questions she could think of.

God helped King Solomon give the right answers every time. He explained many things the queen did not understand.

"Everything I heard about you is true," the queen told King Solomon.

After the queen talked to King Solomon, she took a walk around the palace. She had never in all her life seen anything like it. The food was delicious. The house was gorgeous. The service was wonderful. And even the servants were dressed in beautiful clothes.

"King Solomon," the queen said, "I heard that you were the wisest man who ever lived. I heard that you were rich. But you are twice as rich and twice as wise as I heard you were. I didn't believe it was possible until I came. Now I have seen it for myself.

"Your people are blessed to have such a wise leader," said the queen. "Thanks be to the Lord your God who made you king over Israel. Your God loves you and your people very much."

Before the queen left to go back to Sheba, she

gave King Solomon the gifts she had brought with her: gold and spices and beautiful jewels.

And she gave him another very special gift, some wood. King Solomon had never seen such beautiful wood. He used the wood to make his house and the house of God even more beautiful. And some of it was used to make harps for his musicians.

Then King Solomon gave the queen some gifts. She had seen many wonderful things as she looked around. And whatever she wanted, he gave her.

The queen of Sheba was not the only person who came to see King Solomon. Many people came from all over the world. Some came to see his beautiful throne of ivory and gold. Some came to see his golden cups and plates. Some came to ask him questions and to hear him speak. Some came to see his 1400 chariots and his 12,000 horsemen.

And everyone who came brought gifts. They brought gold and silver and ivory and apes and peacocks and clothing and weapons and spices and horses and mules.

Solomon was very rich and very wise. But he was very foolish in an important thing. As he got older, he began to worship idols. He was no longer happy. His people began to fight one another. Without God, all of his riches were no good.

EKEL
PHARSIN

Choices

HP.

Two Builders

"Did you hear what I said?" asked Bob's father.

"Yes, Dad," Bob answered. "You said I should never play near the railroad tracks."

Bob did hear what his father said. But he has a choice. He can obey or he can disobey.

Jesus sometimes told stories about people and the choices they made. One story was about two builders.

The first builder hunted for a big flat rock on which to build his house. He didn't want to be afraid when the storms came that his house would wash away. He finally found just the right rock in just the right place. So he got his building mate-

rials and tools, and built his house on the rock.

The second builder was not so careful. He knew that storms sometimes came. But he saw a sandy spot with a lovely view of the sea. And he built his house there on the sand.

Then one day, sure enough, a storm came. The rain fell, and flooding started. Strong winds blew against the two houses.

The house built on the rock lost a few shingles, but it stood firm against the storm. The house built on the sand fell.

Jesus said that everyone who hears His words and obeys them is like the wise man who built his house on the rock. Those who hear His words but do not obey are foolish—like the man who chose to build his house on the sand.

Long Live the King!

Everybody liked David. That is, everybody except King Saul liked him. And King Saul was jealous, so jealous that he was looking for David to kill him.

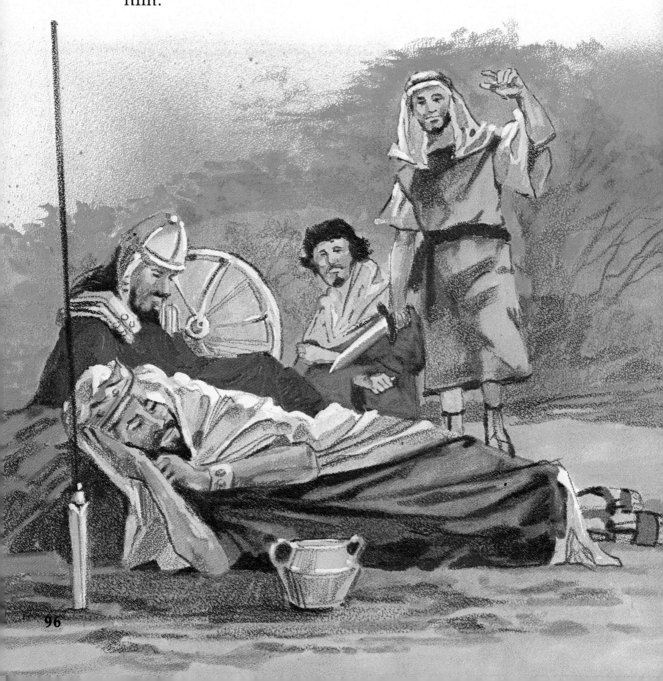

While King Saul kept hunting David, David chose not to harm the king. One time David cut off a piece of the king's robe as the king lay sleeping to prove that he could have killed him. But Saul still wanted to kill David.

Another time, David was hiding in the wilderness near Ziph, when the Ziphites told Saul where he was. Saul hurried after him with 3,000 of his best troops. When it got dark, and they had not found David, they camped beside the road.

Now David knew where Saul was. He decided to take a friend and go down to Saul's campground.

"Who wants to go along?" David asked.

"I'll go," said Abishai.

So David and Abishai quietly entered Saul's

camp. In the dark they could see King Saul asleep in the middle of the sleeping soldiers. His spear* was stuck in the ground at his head. Even General Abner was asleep.

"Here's our chance to kill him," Abishai whispered to David. "Let me pin him to the ground with his own spear. One stroke will do it!"

"No," said David. "I won't choose to kill him. He is still God's chosen king. God will take care of him. Perhaps he will die in battle or in old age. But I won't be the one to kill him."

As David looked at Saul and the soldiers sleeping, he had an idea. "Let's take Saul's spear and water jug and leave," he said.

As soon as David and his friend were a good distance away on top of the mountain, David called, "Abner!"

Saul's general replied, "Who's calling?"

"Why didn't you guard King Saul? Somebody came in to kill the king while you were asleep. Can you find the king's spear? Where is his water jug?"

The king recognized David's voice. "Is that you, David?" he called.

"Yes," said David. "Why do you keep chasing me? What have I done?"

Saul was ashamed. "I've done wrong, David," Saul said. "You spared my life today. I won't try to hurt you anymore."

"I have your spear," David said. "Send somebody over to get it. The Lord rewards people who make right choices. I could have killed you, but I didn't. I respect the Lord. I pray that He will take care of me."

Then Saul said to David, "May God bless you. You will do many great things."

Saul and David parted, each going his own way. David was blessed by God. And he became the next king of Israel.

The Hand Writing
on the Wall

Suppose you went to a dinner, and suddenly you
saw a hand, all by itself, writing words on a wall.
This is what happened to Belshazzar, king of

Babylon. King Belshazzar was having a big dinner for more than a thousand people. He ordered his servants to bring the gold dishes that had been taken from the temple in Jerusalem. Belshazzar wanted his family and friends to eat and drink from them with him.

When the cups came, Belshazzar and his friends poured wine in the cups and drank it. And they gave thanks to gods of gold and silver and iron and stone and wood, which were not really gods at all.

Suddenly the fingers of a man's hand appeared, writing on the wall. When the king saw the hand,

he got pale. He shook so much his knees knocked together.

"Go get my wise men," he ordered. The wise men came. "If anyone can read the writing and tell what it means, I will give him beautiful clothes and a gold chain for his neck. He will be made the third greatest person in my kingdom."

But the wise men could not even read the words. And certainly no one knew what they meant.

Finally the Queen Mother came in. "I know a man who can read the writing," she said. "When your father lived, this man showed wisdom and goodness. Your father put him over all of the wise men of the kingdom. Daniel can tell the meaning of dreams. Call him."

Daniel was sent for, and came before the king. "Keep your gifts, O King," Daniel said. "But I will tell you what the words mean. The Most High God gave glory and power to your father. But when he became proud and forgot God, he was made to live outside with wild animals. He had to learn that God rules over men and puts whoever He wants on the throne.

"You, O King, knew about your father. Still, you acted like you were greater than God. You took bowls and cups from God's own house and ate and drank from them. And you worshipped idols. For this reason, the hand wrote on the wall. The words

mean, 'God has counted your kingdom and ended it. God has judged you. He will divide your kingdom and give it to the Medes and Persians.' "

Daniel's words made the king tremble. But he kept his promise. He put a gold chain around Daniel's neck. He ordered fine clothes for Daniel and made him the third ruler of the kingdom.

That night the words of Daniel, the man of God, came true. The Medes attacked. Belshazzar, the king who sinned against God, was killed. And Darius, a Mede, became the new king.

Jesus and the Devil

Everybody has choices to make. Often we choose between two good things—like whether to have apple pie or cherry pie. But sometimes we must choose between good and bad.

If somebody tries to get you to choose a wrong thing, he is tempting you. He may make the choice

hard by promising something nice. He may say you'll have more friends. He may say "everybody does it."

Even Jesus was tempted. Here's what happened.

Jesus was ready to start preaching and telling people about God, His Father. But before He began, He had to pass a hard test. He had to choose between good and bad.

First, Jesus was taken into the wilderness and left all alone. He had nothing to eat for forty days and forty nights. You can imagine how hungry and weak He was!

And who should appear? Yes, the devil, the tempter himself.

"I'll bet you could use something to eat!" the devil said to Jesus. "If you are the Son of God, why don't you change these stones into loaves of bread?"

But Jesus was too smart to fall for that!

"God's Word tells us that having something to eat isn't the most important thing in life," He said. "It's much more important to obey God."

The devil could see he would have to try harder if he was going to get Jesus to give in. He had another idea.

This time the devil took Jesus to the top of a very tall building, the temple in Jerusalem.

"If you really are the Son of God, I dare you to jump off. You won't get hurt. God's angels will catch you. It's a good chance to get people to notice you!"

Jesus was the Son of God. There were times in His life when angels came to care for Him. But He would not listen to the devil.

"No way," Jesus answered. "God has not given Me power so I can show off or use it to do foolish things. God's Word says not to tempt Him."

The devil had failed again. Now he took Jesus to a very high mountain. From that spot they could see the whole world.

"You can be the king over everything," the devil promised. "Wouldn't it be wonderful to have everyone in the world thinking you're the greatest?

They'd do everything you say. You would be famous. It's all yours—if you'll worship me!"

"Get out of here, Satan!*" Jesus commanded. "God's Word says He is the only one we should worship and serve."

Then the devil gave up. He could see that his tempting tricks wouldn't work. Jesus knew what God wanted Him to do. And He always obeyed God. He always picked good, never bad. So the devil went away—at least for now.

Suddenly angels did come and take care of Jesus! Jesus had proved that He was God's Son.

The Boy
Who Ran Away

Jesus often told stories to teach a lesson. He told
this story about a father and his two sons.

The younger son decided that he was tired of working with his older brother on the farm.

"Dad," he said one day, "I want my share of your money." So the father divided everything between the two sons.

The younger brother took his money and went away to a foreign country. There he wasted all his money on foolish things.

When he had spent the last of his money, he realized the country was in a bad shape. There was not much food. Lots of people were short of money, and jobs were hard to find. The only job he could get was working for a farmer who raised pigs. He was so hungry that even the food he was giving the pigs looked good to him.

Finally the boy said to himself, "What am I doing here? Even my father's servants have plenty to eat. I have done wrong to my father and against God. I'm not good enough to be a son, but I'll ask my father to treat me as one of his servants." And he started the long walk home.

One day as the father looked across the fields, he couldn't believe his eyes. His wish had come true! His son was coming home.

The father ran to meet his boy. "My son!" he said as he hugged and kissed him.

"I have done wrong," the boy said. "I don't deserve to be called your son."

But the father wasn't listening. "Bring the boy some good clothes," he told his servants. "Get him shoes and bring a ring for his finger! Kill a beef, and let's have a party! I thought my son was dead, but he is alive!"

Now the older son had been working in the field. As he came home, he heard music and the noise of the party.

"What's going on?" he asked a servant.

"Your brother is home!" the servant told him.

"Your father is so happy that we're having a party for him."

Instead of being glad, the older brother was angry. He wouldn't even go into the house. When the father heard what was going on, he went out and begged him to come in.

"Why should I?" the older son shouted. "I've obeyed you and worked all this time, and you've never had a party for me and my friends."

"Son," he said, "you've been here all along. And everything I have is yours, but we need to be happy. We thought your brother was dead. But he's alive! He was lost. And now he's found!"

Who in this story made wrong choices? Who made a right choice?

Esther
Saves Her People

The king of Persia invited his friends to a party at the palace. They were having a good time when the king ordered his servants to bring the queen in so everybody could see how beautiful she was. To the king's surprise, the queen would not come. The king was angry.

"Get a new queen," said his friends.

"Yes," said the king, "that's what I'll do."

The king's friends had another idea. "Let's bring all the beautiful young girls in the kingdom to the palace," they said. "The king can choose the one he likes best to be the new queen." This pleased the king, and he ordered it done.

Now Mordecai, a Jew, lived in the kingdom. And with him lived Esther, his beautiful cousin. When the king's servants came looking for beautiful girls, they took Esther to the palace along with the other young women.

The servant who cared for the girls saw that Esther was lovely. He gave her the nicest place to stay and the best food.

No one at the palace knew Esther was a Jew. Mordecai had told her not to tell. When the king saw Esther, he loved her more than all the others. He made her the queen.

One day Mordecai heard that two of the king's servants planned to kill the king. Mordecai told Esther, who told the king. The men were hanged, and the king's servants wrote it in his book.

Sometime later, the king made a man named Haman ruler over all the princes of the kingdom. All the king's men bowed to Haman, all except Mordecai. That made Haman angry. When he found out Mordecai was a Jew, he decided to get rid of all Jews, and of course, Mordecai.

So Haman went to the king. "There are people in your kingdom who are different from us," he said. "They do not obey you. Give the command to kill them."

This pleased the king, and he gave the command. All Jews, young and old, must die.

When Mordecai heard the command, he and all the other Jews wept. Esther's servants came and told her what was happening. So she sent a servant

to ask Mordecai what was wrong. Mordecai told the servant the whole story. "Tell her she must go to the king, and ask for the lives of our people, the Jews," he said.

Esther sent word back that she could not go before the king unless he sent for her. Anyone who went without being called would be killed—unless the king held out his golden rod.

"Give Esther this message," Mordecai told the servant. "Don't you know if the Jews are killed, you will be killed too? This may be why you were made queen."

Esther was as brave as she was beautiful. "Tell Mordecai to tell all the Jews not to eat or drink anything for three days," she told her servant. "Then I will go to the king. If I die, I die."

After three days, Esther dressed in beautiful clothes and went to see the king. When the king saw her, he held out the golden rod. "What do you want, Queen Esther?" he asked. "I will give you anything, even half of my kingdom."

Esther asked him to bring Haman to a dinner she would prepare. So that night the king and Haman went to the dinner, and the king asked Esther again what she wanted. She did not answer, but invited him and Haman to dinner the next night. "Next time," she told the king, "I will tell you."

Haman was happy to be invited again, but when he saw Mordecai, who still would not bow to him, he was very angry. "Tomorrow," he said, "I'll ask the king to hang that Jew."

That night the king could not sleep, so he asked a servant to read from his book to him. The servant read about the time Mordecai saved the king's life. "Did we reward Mordecai?" the king asked. "No," the servant answered.

The king ordered Haman to put the king's clothes on Mordecai and lead him through town on the king's horse. "Tell everyone," the king ordered, "this is the man who pleases the king."

Poor Haman. He had to obey. That night, as he went to the queen's dinner, he felt terrible.

"Now, my Queen," the king said, after they had eaten. "Tell me what you wish."

"If you care about me," Esther said, "do not let me be killed. My people and I are all going to be killed."

"Who dares do such a thing?" the king cried.

"That man," Esther said as she pointed to Haman. Haman was hanged, and Mordecai was chosen to take Haman's place with the king.

The Jews were spared because Queen Esther was willing to risk her life to save her people.

Favorite Chapters of the Bible

The Beginning

In the beginning God created the heavens and the earth. Now the earth was formless and empty, darkness was over the surface of the deep, and the Spirit of God was hovering over the waters.

And God said, "Let there be light," and there was light. God saw that the light was good, and he separated the light from the darkness. God called the light "day" and the darkness he called "night." And there was evening, and there was morning the first day.

And God said, "Let there be an expanse between the waters to separate water from water." So God made the expanse and separated the water under the expanse from the water above it. And it was so. God called the expanse "sky." And there was evening, and there was morning the second day.

Genesis 1:1-8

The Beatitudes

Now when he saw the crowds, he went up on a mountainside and sat down. His disciples came to him, and he began to teach them, saying:
"Blessed are the poor in spirit,
   for theirs is the kingdom of heaven.
Blessed are those who mourn,
   for they will be comforted.
Blessed are the meek,
   for they will inherit the earth.
Blessed are those who hunger and thirst
   for righteousness,
   for they will be filled.
Blessed are the merciful,
   for they will be shown mercy.
Blessed are the pure in heart,
   for they will see God.
Blessed are the peacemakers,
   for they will be called sons of God.
Blessed are those who are persecuted
   because of righteousness,
   for theirs is the kingdom of heaven.
Blessed are you when people insult you, persecute you and falsely say all kinds of evil against you because of me. Rejoice and be glad, because great is your reward in heaven, for in the same way they persecuted the prophets who were before you."

Matthew 5:1-12

Jesus and the Children

People were bringing little children to Jesus to have him touch them, but the disciples rebuked them. When Jesus saw this, he was indignant. He said to them, "Let the little children come to me, and do not hinder them, for the kingdom of God belongs to such as these. I tell you the truth, anyone who will not receive the kingdom of God like a little child will never enter it." And he took the children in his arms, put his hands on them and blessed them. *Mark 10:13-16*

Psalm 100

Shout for joy to the Lord, all the earth.
Serve the Lord with gladness;
come before him with joyful songs.
Know that the Lord is God.
It is he who made us, and we are his;
we are his people, the sheep of his pasture.
Enter his gates with thanksgiving
and his courts with praise;
give thanks to him and praise his name.
For the Lord is good
and his love endures forever;
his faithfulness continues through all generations.

The Good Shepherd

"I am the good shepherd. The good shepherd lays down his life for the sheep. The hired hand is not the shepherd who owns the sheep. So when he sees the wolf coming, he abandons the sheep and runs away. Then the wolf attacks the flock and scatters it. The man runs away because he is a hired hand and cares nothing for the sheep.

"I am the good shepherd; I know my sheep and my sheep know me—just as the Father knows me and I know the Father—and I lay down my life for the sheep. I have other sheep that are not of this sheep pen. I must bring them also. They too will listen to my voice, and there shall be one flock and one shepherd. The reason my Father loves me is that I lay down my life—only to take it up again. No one takes it from me, but I lay it down of my own accord. I have authority to lay it down and authority to take it up again. This command I received from my Father."

These words of Jesus are found in John 10:11-18

God Gave His Son

Now there was a man of the Pharisees named Nicodemus, a member of the Jewish ruling council. He came to Jesus at night and said, "Rabbi, we know you are a teacher who has come from God. For no one could perform the miraculous signs you are doing if God were not with him."

In reply Jesus declared, "I tell you the truth, unless a man is born again, he cannot see the kingdom of God."

"How can a man be born when he is old?" Nicodemus asked. "Surely he cannot enter a second time into his mother's womb to be born!"

Jesus answered, "I tell you the truth, unless a man is born of water and the Spirit, he cannot enter the kingdom of God. Flesh gives birth to flesh, but the Spirit gives birth to spirit. You should not be surprised at my saying, 'You must be born again.'

"For God so loved the world that he gave his one and only Son, that whoever believes in him shall not perish but have eternal life. For God did not send his Son into the world to condemn the world, but to save the world through him."

John 3:1-7, 16, 17

Jesus Is Coming Back Again

"When the Son of Man comes in his glory, and all the angels with him, he will sit on his throne in heavenly glory. All the nations will be gathered before him, and he will separate the people one from another as a shepherd separates the sheep from the goats. He will put the sheep on his right and the goats on his left.

"Then the King will say to those on his right, 'Come, you who are blessed by my Father; take your inheritance, the kingdom prepared for you since the creation of the world. For I was hungry and you gave me something to eat, I was thirsty and you gave me something to drink, I was a stranger and you invited me in, I needed clothes and you clothed me, I was sick and you looked after me, I was in prison and you came to visit me.'

"Then the righteous will answer him, 'Lord, when did we see you hungry and feed you, or thirsty and give you something to drink? When did we see you a stranger and invite you in, or needing clothes and clothe you? When did we see you sick or in prison and go to visit you?'

"The King will reply, 'I tell you the truth, whatever you did for one of the least of these brothers of mine, you did for me.' "   *Matthew 25:31-40*

Heaven

Then I saw a new heaven and a new earth, for the first heaven and the first earth had passed away, and there was no longer any sea. I saw the Holy City, the new Jerusalem, coming down out of heaven from God, prepared as a bride beautifully dressed for her husband. And I heard a loud voice from the throne saying, ''Now the dwelling of God is with men, and he will live with them. They will be his people, and God himself will be with them and be their God. He will wipe every tear from their eyes. There will be no more death or mourning or crying or pain, for the old order of things has passed away.''

The city does not need the sun or the moon to shine on it, for the glory of God gives it light, and the Lamb is its lamp. The nations will walk by its light, and the kings of the earth will bring their splendor into it. On no day will its gates ever be shut, for there will be no night there. The glory and honor of the nations will be brought into it. Nothing impure will ever enter it, nor will anyone who does what is shameful or deceitful, but only those whose names are written in the Lamb's book of life. *Revelation 21:1-4, 23-27*

When You Pray

When you pray, go into your room, close the door and pray to your Father, who is unseen. Then your Father, who sees what is done in secret, will reward you. And when you pray, do not keep on babbling like pagans, for they think they will be heard because of their many words. Do not be like them, for your Father knows what you need before you ask him.

This is how you should pray:
"Our Father in heaven,
hallowed be your name,
your kingdom come,
your will be done
on earth as it is in heaven.
Give us today our daily bread.
Forgive us our debts,
as we also have forgiven our debtors.
And lead us not into temptation,
but deliver us from the evil one."

For if you forgive men when they sin against you, your heavenly Father will also forgive you. But if you do not forgive men their sins, your Father will not forgive your sins.

Matthew 6:6-15

Some Proverbs

Trust in the Lord with all your heart and lean not on your own understanding; in all your ways acknowledge him, and he will make your paths straight (3:5, 6).

A wise son brings joy to his father (10:1).

He who walks with the wise grows wise, but a companion of fools suffers harm (13:20).

Righteousness exalts a nation, but sin is a disgrace to any people (14:34).

Pride goes before destruction, a haughty spirit before a fall (16:18).

Better a patient man than a warrior, a man who controls his temper than one who takes a city (16:32).

A friend loves at all times (17:17).

A good name is more desirable than great riches; to be esteemed is better than silver or gold (22:1).

Train a child in the way he should go, and when he is old he will not turn from it (22:6).

Do not answer a fool according to his folly, or you will be like him yourself (26:4).

Without gossip a quarrel dies down (26:20).

Do not boast about tomorrow, for you do not know what a day may bring forth (27:1).

Let another praise you, and not your own mouth (27:2).

Glossary

altar. A table, mount, or other construction of turf, wood, stone or metal, on which sacrifice was made to God or an idol. The first altar mentioned in the Bible is the one built by Noah.

baptized. Dipped under the water. A person who is baptized in Christ shows that he is a follower of Christ.

blessed. Favored in a special way. God has blessed certain people and nations by doing special things for them. People can bless God by expressing thankfulness for His goodness and power.

booth. Huts made of branches of trees and other things. Booths are made to last for only a short time.

chariot. A cart or wagon pulled by a horse or horses.

Christians. People who believe that Jesus is the Christ the Son of God and who try to obey His commandments.

convertible. A car with a top that can be rolled back.

crucified. Put to death by hanging on a cross. The hands and feet were fastened to the cross, and the person left there until he was dead.

desert. A place in which there are no people living.

disciple. A person who listens to and follows someone.

disease. A sickness or illness.

earthquake. A trembling of a part of the earth. Big cracks sometimes form in the earth. Sometimes rocks are thrown in the air. An earthquake in Jerusalem once caused the death of 10,000 people.

herbs. Small plants that are used for medicine or food.

Hosanna. A shout of praise to God similar to our saying, "Praise the Lord."

Israelites. The Jews; children, grandchildren, great grandchildren, etc., of Jacob; God's chosen people.

lice. Little bugs that live on animals, people, or plants. They suck the blood of animals and people, and the juices of plants.

locusts. Grasshoppers or beetles that eat every green thing in their way. They sometimes go into houses and eat the woodwork.

miracles. Wonderful things that can be done only by God, by God's Son, or by someone to whom God has given special power.

pomegranates. Thick-skinned reddish berries the size of an orange. They have lots of seeds, red pulp, and an acid flavor.

popularity. The state of being well-liked and well-known by many people.

prophet. A person who speaks for someone else, especially God. He may be able to tell things that will happen at some future time.

resurrection. The coming to life again from the dead.

sacrifices. Offerings of animals, food, etc., to God or an idol as an act of thanksgiving.

Satan. Another name for the devil, the enemy of God and Jesus.

savior. A person who saves people from something. Jesus Christ is our Savior because He saves us from sin and hell.

slaves. People who are under the control of someone else and must do whatever that person tells them to do. They are usually made to do the hard work.

spear. A long sharp-pointed weapon used to kill people and animals.

spirit. The breath of life which God breathed into man at the creation. This is the part of men and women that is different from the animals. The Holy Spirit was with God and Jesus when they made the world. Jesus called Him "the Comforter." He helps Christians understand God's Word and do what God wants them to do.

sword. A weapon with a handle and a very sharp blade.

tabernacle. A special tent that was made to be God's house. It was carried with the Israelites when they traveled from one place to another. When they camped, they put the tabernacle in the center of the camp.

thrilled. Very excited.

tribe. A group of families who live close together.

village. A small town.

wilderness. A wild land in which there are no people and no crops.